Every Drop Counts

Anita Nahta Amin

Reader Consultants

Jennifer M. Lopez, M.S.Ed., NBCT
Senior Coordinator—History/Social Studies
Norfolk Public Schools

Tina Ristau, M.A., SLMS
Teacher Librarian
Waterloo Community School District

iCivics Consultants

Emma Humphries, Ph.D.
Chief Education Officer

Taylor Davis, M.T.
Director of Curriculum and Content

Natacha Scott, MAT
Director of Educator Engagement

Publishing Credits

Rachelle Cracchiolo, M.S.Ed., *Publisher*
Emily R. Smith, M.A.Ed., *VP of Content Development*
Véronique Bos, *Creative Director*
Dona Herweck Rice, *Senior Content Manager*
Dani Neiley, *Associate Content Specialist*
Fabiola Sepulveda, *Series Designer*
Hanah McCaffery, *Illustrator, pages 6–9*

Image Credits: p13 NASA; p15 USDA Photo by Lance Cheung; p17 NASA; p22 AFP/Stringer/Getty Images; all other images from iStock and/or Shutterstock

Library of Congress Cataloging-in-Publication Data

Names: Amin, Anita Nahta, author.
Title: Every drop counts / Anita Nahta Amin.
Description: Huntington Beach, CA : Teacher Created Materials, [2021] | Includes index. | Audience: Grades 2-3 | Summary: "Water seems to be everywhere. Yet, the world is running out of fresh water. How does this affect lives around the world? What has been done and what more can we do to try and escape this disaster?"-- Provided by publisher.
Identifiers: LCCN 2020043589 (print) | LCCN 2020043590 (ebook) | ISBN 9781087604992 (paperback) | ISBN 9781087620015 (ebook)
Subjects: LCSH: Water-supply--Juvenile literature.
Classification: LCC TD348 .A45 2021 (print) | LCC TD348 (ebook) | DDC 333.91/16--dc23
LC record available at https://lccn.loc.gov/2020043589
LC ebook record available at https://lccn.loc.gov/2020043590

TCM Teacher Created Materials
5482 Argosy Avenue
Huntington Beach, CA 92649-1039
www.tcmpub.com

ISBN 978-1-0876-0499-2

Table of Contents

The Last Drop

It may seem as if water will never run out. It covers more than two-thirds of Earth. But most of that water is salty. It is not **fresh water**. Fresh water is what we use to drink, wash clothes, bathe, and water the lawn.

For every one hundred drops of water on Earth, only three are fresh. This means a small amount of all the world's water is safe to drink. Some places have more fresh water than others.

But what if there is no more water to use? Many people are facing this problem now. And many more might face it later.

Jump into Fiction

A River Runs Dry

Tina's plants are droopy. She is not happy. She had imagined a lush garden.

Mom sighs, "We need rain."

Back inside, Dad waves a newspaper. "Crystal River is drying up! We have to save water."

"But my plants!" Tina cries.

"Our town could become a desert," Mom says.

Tina starts to make changes. She turns off the tap while brushing her teeth. She shortens her showers. She uses leftover cooking water for her plants.

"Every drop counts!" Mom says. Her plants perk up with pasta water.

A week later, Dad reads the front page of the newspaper. "The river is still shrinking. Keep saving water."

Tina runs outside. "Mr. Sand, please don't water your lawn!" She makes flyers to remind every neighbor.

A week later, the newspaper praises Tina's flyer. It says that she is helping to save Crystal River!

Tina beams. Then, she feels a drop on her face. "Look! It's raining!" Tina takes a pail outside to catch rainwater. The river is safe for now. But she isn't taking chances with the future!

Back to Nonfiction

Water Around the World

Someone turns on a **tap**. *Whooshhh!* Water comes pouring out, but from where? It may have flowed through pipes from far away.

Most tap water comes from lakes or rivers. It also comes from special human-made pools that collect rain and melted snow. Water can come from wells and springs too. Most of the time, many people share these water sources.

But much of the world can't get tap water at home. People share public taps or walk to fetch water from wells, springs, or rivers.

Public Water in Ancient Rome

Ancient Romans got their water from distant places. Water flowed from hills down to towns. It flowed through linked tunnels and bridges called *aqueducts*.

Think and Talk

Why is water so important to everyone?

Scientists think less rain will fall over time. By 2025, half of the world won't have fresh water. **Climate change** will bring hotter days. **Droughts** will get worse. More lakes and rivers will dry up.

a dried up river bed in Nepal

In **struggling** communities, water can be unsafe. It may have germs that could make people sick. Some people dump trash and chemicals in rivers. This also makes the water dirty. Yet the world keeps growing with more people born each year. And those people need fresh water.

Aral Sea in Asia, 2000

Aral Sea in Asia, 2014

The Most Fresh Water

Brazil, Russia, and the United States have the most fresh water in the world. But they have less than they used to. Droughts have caused some water sources to dry up.

Help Wanted: Water Heroes

How can the water problem be solved? No one knows for sure. Scientists, leaders, and citizens are all trying to help. They are working to find answers and make changes.

People are looking for new water sources. New tools might help make more usable water. People can also use less water so it lasts longer, or they can reuse water. Some of these changes are easier than others. Some cost more. But it's important to keep trying.

A worker checks a water filter system.

Water flows through small tubes to save water.

Think and Talk

How might watering plants as shown in the picture help save water?

Finding Water

A lot of water hides under the ground in **aquifers**. Rain pools into these spaces. People drill wells to look for the pooled rain. When this water is used up, it can take a thousand years to refill!

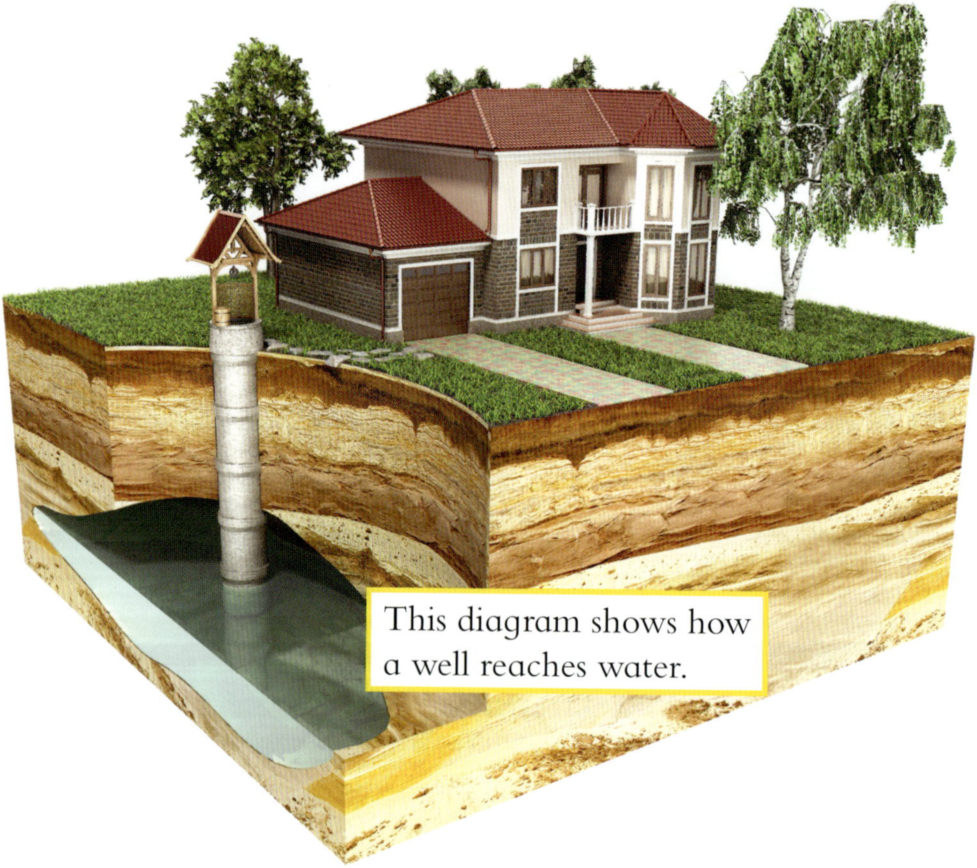

This diagram shows how a well reaches water.

NASA can also help find water. **Satellites** keep track of the world's water. They see how much water is in the air, on the ground, and under the ground. They can help predict when the next drought may start. This helps people plan better.

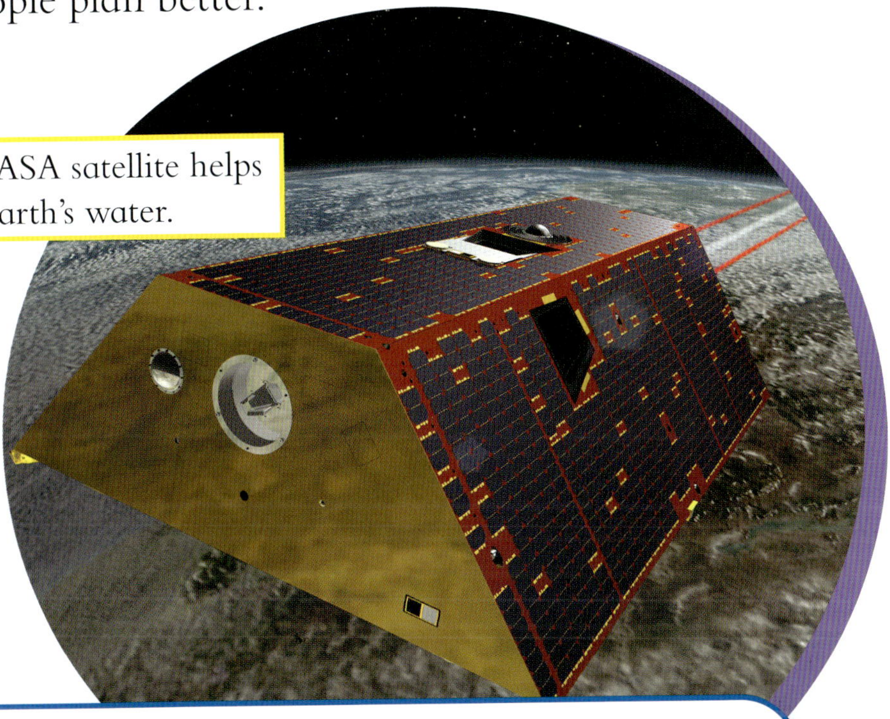

This NASA satellite helps track Earth's water.

Unsafe Water

Dirty water can make people sick. Nearly one billion people in the world do not have clean water. That is about one out of every eight people in the world!

Saving Water

In a drought, communities may limit water use. Some easy things can help save water. For example, you can fix leaks. A leak can waste thousands of gallons (liters) of water each year. Also, you can shut off the tap when brushing your teeth. You could save a lot of water in this way. And you can take short showers. You can get clean in under five minutes!

Fixing leaky faucets can help save water.

Outside, you can grow only plants that need little water. In fact, some countries will not grow thirsty plants, such as cotton. If your lawn needs more than rain, a lawn where you live may not be a good idea.

Who Owns Rain?

Rain barrels collect rainwater. In all but two states, people can collect and use as much rainwater as they want. Rainwater can be used to water plants, for cleaning, and more.

Reusing Water

Oceans cover the world, but people can't drink salt water. The salt only makes them thirstier. Some factories take the salt out of seawater. The water becomes fresh! But the salt is pumped back into the sea. Now there is suddenly more salt in the water. This can hurt the animals there.

Some places clean **wastewater**. Factories clean the water. They take out dirt, oils, germs, and more. They make the water ready for people to drink and use. But cleaning can be costly and uses energy.

This factory in Germany takes salt out of water.

Making Water

Pulling water out of air might sound like a magic trick. But engineers have found some ways to do it. A special machine can cool warm air to make drops. A net can be used to catch fog. A bottle with a net can fill itself with water.

A scientist tests a sample of water.

People are trying to make rain with small metal seeds. They shoot them into the sky. Water in the air sticks to the seeds. This makes clouds form. Then, it rains. Scientists don't know yet how well these seeds will work.

Drinking Fog

The beetles in the Namib Desert drink fog. Bumps on their wings catch fog and turn the fog into water drops. The drops slide down into their mouths.

More Than Gold

The earliest towns were formed on the banks of rivers. The people needed water to grow food, to fish, and to drink. But there were droughts too. So they caught rain in clay pools.

Water was important then. And it still is. In the driest places, people may fight over water. Countries may fight too.

Water can be worth more than gold. Every drop counts for people who don't have enough water. To them, and to the world, water is priceless.

World Water Day

World Water Day is on March 22 each year. People learn more about fresh water and how to preserve it.

Glossary

aquifers—groups of underground rocks with spaces in between to store rain

climate change—unusual changes in global or area climate patterns over time

droughts—periods of time with little or no rain

fresh water—water without salt

NASA—National Aeronautics and Space Administration; a U.S. group in charge of exploring space

satellites—human-made machines that move around Earth in space

struggling—dealing with many severe challenges

tap—faucet

wastewater—used water from drains, such as sinks, showers, and toilets

Index

Civics in Action

You can make a difference in the way people use water. Make a plan to help your family and neighbors save water along with you.

1. Explain the world's water shortage.
2. List ways people can help.
3. Present your ideas to other classes.
4. Talk to friends and neighbors.
5. Have people tell you how they will change what they do.